Giving as an Act of Worship

Michael A. Milton, Ph. D.

Faith for Living

Bible Messages

Wipf and Stock Publishers
Eugene, Oregon

Wipf and Stock Publishers
199 West 8th Avenue, Suite 3
Eugene OR 97401

Giving as an Act of Worship
By Michael A. Milton, Ph. D.

1st edition.
Printed in the United States of America

ISBN: 1-59752-712-2

Faith for Living
Bible Messages

The booklet you are reading is part of a series of Bible messages on select topics prepared from sermons I delivered at First Presbyterian Church of Chattanooga, Tennessee. Each of them is designed to address theological issues in the Bible that need to be translated into a "faith for living." It is my belief that all theology is, ultimately and necessarily, practical. Theology that is not practical is not a theology rightly applied. For all theology must, as Dr. Robert L Reymond says, "pass a radical Biblical muster."

> All Scripture is breathed out by God and profitable for teaching, for reproof, for correction, and for training in righ teousness, that the man of God may be competent, equipped for every good work (2 Timothy 3:16-17).

In *Giving As an Act of Worship* I pray that God will encourage, not just your giving, but His glory in your giving.

This little booklet is dedicated to the glory of Jesus Christ and produced in honor of the congregation I serve at First Presbyterian Church of Chattanooga, Tennessee.

Giving as an Act of Worship

Philippians 4:10-20

Under what category in the church would you place the act of giving? Under financial stewardship? Maybe. Perhaps under "Things we know we have to do, but hate to talk about"? Would you believe that the Bible teaches that giving is on a par with singing hymns and praying and offering thanks?

> I rejoiced in the Lord greatly that now at length you have revived your concern for me. You were indeed concerned for me, but you had no opportunity. Not that I am speaking of being in need, for I have learned in whatever situation I am to be content. I know how to be brought low, and I know how to abound. In any and every circumstance, I have learned the secret of facing plenty and hunger, abundance and need. I can do all things through him who strengthens me. Yet it was kind of you to share my trouble. And you Philippians yourselves know that in the beginning of the gospel, when I left Macedonia, no church entered into partnership with me in giving and receiving, except you only. Even in Thessalonica you sent me help for my needs once and again. Not that I seek the gift, but I seek the fruit that increases to your credit. I have received full payment, and more. I am well supplied, having received from Epaphroditus the gifts you sent, a fragrant offering, a sacrifice acceptable and pleasing to God. And my God will supply every need of yours according to his riches in glory in Christ Jesus. To our God and Father be glory forever and ever. Amen (Philippians 4:10-20).

Step Right Up

Do you remember going to the fair as a child? Remember the color and the strangeness of it all? Remember the "carnies" trying to prod you to spend your money at their amusement? Those cartoon-looking characters would say, "Step right up," and then promise you one of those big, cuddly, stuffed bears if you would only plop down your quarters and dollars. You would give in and lose it all, feeling like a complete sucker. As you watched the carnie spinning his pitch for the next unsuspecting victim, you felt like yelling, "Watch out! This isn't all it's cracked up to be!"

May I make a confession to you? I feel like that when I watch certain religious television shows trying to get money. They promise prayer cloths and special blessings if you will just "step right up." You send a check and you know what happens? The blessing is all...theirs. And you? You become just another pretty name on a mailing list. The whole business of fund-raising in churches can get out of hand.

From the position of a pastor, I hate it. I detest seeing the church act like a carnival sideshow, enticing people into the booth with promises of special blessings if they will just give. However, my concern—and maybe yours—should not cause us to miss an important truth: the church has the obligation to look to her people for tithes and offerings to advance the kingdom of God. Each of us is obliged to give, but in the Bible giving is not just an annual appeal. In the Bible giving is an act of worship.

This truth is taught in several places in Scripture, but one of the clearest examples is found in Philippians 4:18 where the Apostle Paul is thanking the Philippians for their financial gifts. In one statement, Paul brings together all the teaching on giving in the Bible and tells the congregation at Philippi, which had supported Paul, that giving is, in fact, an act of worship. Speaking of their giving, Paul writes that it is "...a fragrant offering, a sacrifice acceptable and pleasing to God."

Giving is an act of worship to God. It may be supporting the work of the local church, it may be sending out missionaries, it may be planting churches, it may be helping to support seminarians who are preparing for the gospel ministry, it may be turning on the lights in the sanctuary week in and week out in order that the gospel may be proclaimed, but we must see that it is something more than this. It is first and foremost an act of worship.

God Does Not Need Our Gifts

If we think we need to give to help God, then we are wrong. Paul tells the Philippians, "Not that I speak in respect of want." And he goes on to say, "I have learned, in whatsoever state I am, *therewith* to be content."[1] Paul knew that God would take care of him.

[1] Philippians 4:11 (KJV)

God will take care of His people and bless His church. The idea that God needs and is dependent on you for His kingdom is bad theology. Israel began to think that God needed them, so the Lord, in a moment of divine sarcasm, spoke to the people of God who had confused the role of sacrifices and giving to the Lord:

> "Hear, O my people, and I will speak;
> O Israel, I will testify against you.
> I am God, your God.
> Not for your sacrifices do I rebuke you;
> your burnt offerings are continually before me.
> I will not accept a bull from your house
> or goats from your folds.
> For every beast of the forest is mine,
> the cattle on a thousand hills.
> I know all the birds of the hills,
> and all that moves in the field is mine.
> "If I were hungry, I would not tell you,
> for the world and its fullness are mine.
> Do I eat the flesh of bulls
> or drink the blood of goats?
> Offer to God a sacrifice of thanksgiving,
> and perform your vows to the Most High,
> and call upon me in the day of trouble;
> I will deliver you, and you shall glorify me" (Psalm 50:7-15).

This is an amazing Psalm. Matthew Henry, the great Puritan Bible commentator, saw this as proof to the carnal Jews that God's glory did not depend on religious ceremony but that those ceremonies were simply instructive of what God would do in reality through Christ.

God does not want our offerings because He is in desperate need of them. God can advance His kingdom without our gifts. He can use a donkey if no man is there to speak. If Israel will not do it, He can cause wise men to journey from afar and bring the gifts He deserves. God's servants, likewise, do not need the gifts. God, who led Abram, who fed Israel with manna, who fed the prophet Elijah with ravens, will take care of those who, like Paul, answer His divine summons to go and tell.

God is bigger than we are. He can take care of Himself. Giving is not an act of sustaining God; it is now and always an act of worship.

However, Paul's teaching on this point does not negate his appreciation for the gift and how it allowed him to continue his work.

God's Will Is That His Work be Advanced Through the Gifts of His People.

> Nevertheless you have done well that you shared in my distress (Philippians 4:14 NKJV).

Again, the Lord could do this another way, but He has chosen this way. Giving was His idea. The offerings of God's people have always been there to support God's work. This is not the work of the government or the marketplace; it is the work of God's people. Paul shows that there are several issues related to this truth.

When we give, we get to share in the burden of God's work.

The Philippian church was made up of ordinary people like you and me. They were laborers, professionals, craftsmen, housewives, students, and little children. They were not called by God to plant churches. God called Paul to do that. But Paul says that they "have done well" as they shared in his distress. They became participants in the ministry of the Apostle Paul.

When you give to the church, you participate in areas of ministry to which you would otherwise have no access. Your gifts share in the burden of taking care of those who serve. Your gifts share in the burden of carrying the message around the community and the globe.

"You have done well" is a commendation that tells me that I do not have to give, I get to give, and there is a remarkable difference between the two.

When we give, we stand in the gap, because many do not give.

> And you Philippians yourselves know that in the beginning of the gospel, when I left Macedonia, no church entered into partnership with me in giving and receiving, except you only (Philippians 4:15).

We give as an act of worship to God and recognize that many do not give. I read that the normal offering for most evangelical Christians is close to 3%. That is worshiping a small God. We should give and, like the Philippians, give greatly because we know that many do not give. They have not matured, they do not appreciate the joy of giving and the blessings of giving, they are new to the faith, or they are lacking in faith, so we give.

Some do not give because they are facing extraordinary circumstances. Many of the churches in Paul's day were new, were struggling, and apparently could not give the way they would later. The church is filled with those people. Thus, those who are able, give more. This is a privilege.

God challenged Ezekiel:

> And I sought for a man among them who should build up the wall and stand in the breach before me for the land, that I should not destroy it, but I found none [Ezekiel 22:30).

Today we have the joy of answering the challenge. We have the opportunity to follow the example of a godly church in Philippi and stand in the gap to advance the gospel of Jesus Christ in our day.

God does not need our gifts but He calls us to give and He uses those gifts to build His kingdom. I have a friend who is a retired missionary who served in Korea. He once told me that when he was planting churches in Korea, he was so called to do it that he would have done it with his own money. If no one had given, the fire inside his bones to see people saved and taught the truth of Christ in a local church would have compelled him to tent-make or even take out a loan to make it happen. "But," he said, "I am thankful for God's people who stood in the gap. It allowed me to focus. It provided the resources I needed to be about the ministry. Souls will be in heaven because someone stood in the gap."

Beloved, we give as an act of worship; and when we do, God's work goes forward. What a great privilege to be Philippian givers!

Giving Is an Act of Worship That Brings Blessings.

There are spiritual blessings for the giver.

> Not that I seek the gift, but I seek the fruit that increases to your credit (Philippians 4:17).

The fruit that abounds to the account of the Philippian givers is spiritual fruit. Dear friend, when you turn to God in prayer to say, "Lord, I am going to worship you with my possessions," something powerful is happening in your soul. You are prioritizing God. You are saying that God owns it all. You are securing for yourself tremendous spiritual blessings which will impact every area of your life. The tree of your life will begin to blossom with new spiritual fruit of contentment, happiness, longsuffering, and peace because giving is an act of worship. When you give, you are, thus, entering into the highest activity of man—to worship God and to enjoy Him. Giving brings spiritual blessings.

Giving brings us into contact with God's providential blessings.

> And my God will supply every need of yours according to his riches in glory in Christ Jesus (Philippians 4:19).

To give is to enter into the worship of God. This, then, is an act that God blesses. This is not a cause-and-effect way to manipulate God into blessing us. It is a spiritual reality that happens when we prioritize God in giving.

Many of us know the familiar passage in Malachi where God challenges Israel to give.

> Bring all the tithes into the storehouse,
> That there may be food in My house... (Malachi 3:10, NKJV).

There is the divine call to worship God with our gift, but here is the motivation for the giver:

> ...And try Me now in this,"
> Says the Lord of hosts,
> "If I will not open for you the windows of heaven
> And pour out for you such blessing
> That there will not be room enough to receive it."
> And I will rebuke the devourer for your sakes,
> So that he will not destroy the fruit of your ground,
> Nor shall the vine fail to bear fruit for you in the field,"
> Says the Lord of hosts;"
> And all nations will call you blessed,
> For you will be a delightful land,"
> Says the Lord of hosts (Malachi 3:10-12, NKJV).

God's providential governing begins to work for the life of the believer who worships Him in this way. I do not want to be that carnie trying to sell that elusive stuffed Teddy bear. I just want you to hear God's invitation to a life of joy, a life of assurance, a life that responds to God in giving and trusts God for His promises. He works all things together for good to those that love Him and are the called according to His purposes. The giving is simply making your calling and election sure. The giving is simply proving your genuineness, and God will take care to fulfill His promises to you.

A father and son were sharing peanuts at a baseball game. Of course, the dad had purchased the peanuts, and the little boy was eating them. The dad asked if he could have some of those peanuts. The little boy drew the bag back and said, "No! These are mine!" The father looked his little boy in the eye and said, "Son, I gave you those nuts. I don't need them, but I was hoping you would share them with me just so we could eat them together." The little boy was old enough to know he was wrong. In fact, his eyes filled with tears and he said, "Oh, Daddy, all of it is yours. You bought them for me, and I was too selfish to share them. Dad, take them all." The father put his arm around the boy. "Son, I don't care about the nuts, I want all of you."

Some of us forget that God owns it all. All that we have came from Him. We selfishly cling to our possessions and say, "No! It's mine!" to our heavenly Father. We think of our gifts, our talents, as our own, and we say, "No! I will not take my vacation to help teach Vacation Bible School!" "No! I will not give of my money to support the church!" Some try to placate their Father and say, "OK, then, one peanut...but no more!" However, when we read about the Philippians, we see how God does not need our money but that it is just an indication of our own heart. Then some of us see the truth of it all: giving is just a way to say, "I love you" to One who loved us first.

Conclusion

The Apostle Paul was constantly under attack, and we may assume that part of the attack had to do with money. Paul associated giving with worship and was not hesitant to bring it up. He did so here, and he did so in 2 Corinthians, where he encourages giving:

> The point is this: whoever sows sparingly will also reap sparingly, and whoever sows bountifully will also reap bountifully. Each one must give as he has made up his mind, not reluctantly or under compulsion, for God loves a cheerful giver (2 Corinthians 9:6-7).

Then Paul brings it back to worship:

> Thanks be to God for his inexpressible gift! (2 Corinthians 9:15).

God does not need our giving. But we need to give, because giving is an act of thanksgiving to God for having called us into His family; an act of adoration for putting the punishment for our sins upon His only begotten Son; an act of praise for filling us with the Holy Spirit; and a hope that, through our giving, others like us, who are in their sins, may be set free and brought into the glorious family of God.

One thing we should make clear—this passage is directed to those who have received God's gift of eternal life through Christ. Paul was reminding the Philippian believers that their financial gift was a sweet smelling sacrifice of praise to the Lord. Your money cannot buy God and it cannot secure blessings.

The promises are given to the person who has received the gift and is now responding to it. The reason we may rejoice in giving is that we have received the greatest gift of all: our sins forgiven, our lives transformed, and God's assurance that when we die we will be with Him forever. And that brings what Jesus called "abundant life." If you have never done that, this message about giving is a challenge for you to receive. To receive that abundant life is to repent of your sins, to recognize your need of a Savior, and to look by faith to Jesus Christ.

Then, having given your life to Christ, you will want to give your all to Him and His kingdom because giving is first and foremost an act of worship of a transformed heart.

EARLY BURIALS

FROM

THE AGORA CEMETERIES

AMERICAN SCHOOL OF CLASSICAL STUDIES
AT ATHENS

PRINCETON, NEW JERSEY

1973

Pelike attributed to the Lykaon Painter: Elpenor, Odysseus, and Hermes. About 440 B.C. Courtesy Museum of Fine Arts, Boston.

'. . . and the souls
of the perished dead gathered to the place, up out of Erebos,
brides and young unmarried men, and long-suffering elders,
virgins, tender with the sorrows of young hearts upon them,
and many fighting men killed in battle, stabbed with brazen
spears, still carrying their bloody armor upon them.'

Odyssey, XI, 36–41

THUS HOMER DESCRIBES some of the shades (*psychai*) whom Odysseus summons from the Underworld when he goes to inquire of Teiresias about his journey back to Ithaca. They were conjured up by an elaborate ceremony, involving a sacrifice to the dead, since once the dead were properly buried they did not consort with the living. Elpenor, the unfortunate companion who fell from the roof of Circe's palace and whose corpse was left behind, was a different case. He was the first to appear, and he pleads and threatens for the burial that was his due:

'there at that time, my Lord. I ask that you remember me,
and do not go and leave me behind unwept, unburied,
when you leave, for fear that I might become the gods' curse upon you;
but burn me there with all my armor that belongs to me,
and heap up a grave mound beside the beach of the gray sea,
for an unhappy man, so that those to come will know of me.'

Odyssey, XI, 71–76

Although the dead buried beneath the Agora cannot speak to us, as Elpenor did to Odysseus, of the proper mode of burial for their given period and station in life, we can observe the burial practices and speculate on the reasons behind them. Some reasons are timeless and still operate in our own funeral practices—grief for the loss of a loved one and the comfort afforded by relatives and friends, the human frailty of wanting to impress others with costliness of offerings or to stress the superior status of the deceased, and the notion that the identity of the individual does not die but should be remembered. However, since the ancient Greeks did not believe in the separation of the 'soul' from the 'body' at the moment of death, they conceived of a journey of the *psyche* to Hades, that could be helped by proper burial rites or hindered by their absence. There was thus fear of the dead. As the shade of Patroklos says to Achilles:

'You sleep, Achilleus; you have forgotten me; but you were not
careless of me when I lived, but only in death. Bury me
as quickly as may be, let me pass through the gates of Hades.
The souls, the images of dead men hold me at a distance,
and will not let me cross the river and mingle among them,
but I wander as I am by Hades' house of the wide gates.'

Iliad, XXIII, 69–74

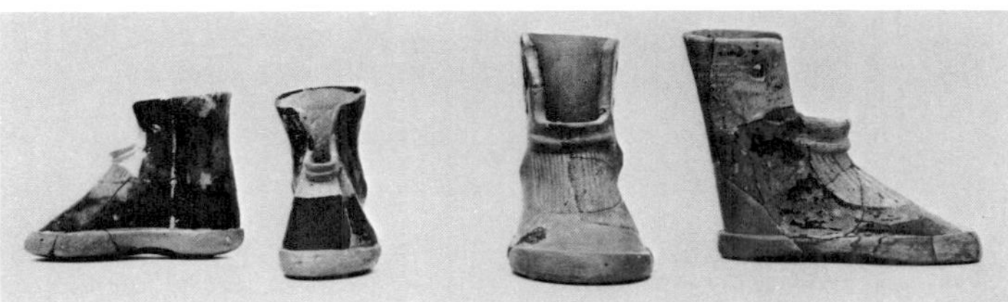

1. Two pairs of terracotta model boots, symbolic equipment for the long journey to the Underworld. From an Early Geometric cremation burial (see 37).

2. North slope of the Areopagus with view of the Acropolis. The wealthiest tombs, both Mycenaean and Geometric, were located here.

Before the constitutional reforms of Solon had created the Agora as a civic center, this region to the northwest of the Acropolis, bounded by the Areopagus and the Pnyx to the south, and the Kolonos Agoraios to the west, was a vast cemetery (see Plan, 6). Over 150 ancient burial places have been discovered by the Agora excavators, but these were only part of the total. With the levelling of the central area for later buildings, many must have been destroyed. Consequently, the best preserved burials are located on the periphery, near the Tholos at the southwest, near the northeast corner and under the Stoa of Attalos (5), and especially along the north side of the Areopagus (2). Because of its proximity to the Acropolis, this last was chosen for tombs of prominent persons in Mycenaean and in Geometric times.

Only one pre-Mycenaean burial has survived, an unusual crouched burial at the bottom of a well shaft near the later Metroon (3). From the two pots associated with the skeleton (4), it can be dated to about 2000 B.C. at the beginning of Middle Helladic (see Chronological Table below Plan, 6).

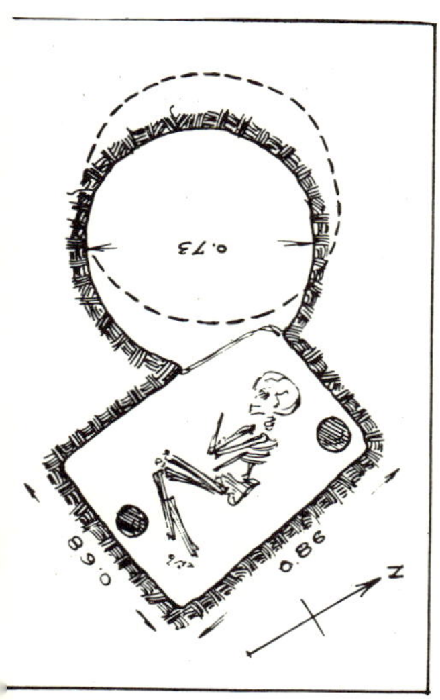

3. Plan of burial of about 2000 B.C.

4. The two pots suggest a belief in an afterlife, or journey to the Other World, for which food was necessary.

5. East side of Agora with Stoa of Attalos. The surviving Mycenaean graves and tombs were especially concentrated at the northeast corner and under the Stoa.

With the Mycenaean period our evidence is much more complete; over forty tombs and graves survive. Many are chamber tombs (7), a type known at Mycenae and elsewhere, but simpler forms also exist (26, 34), perhaps because the geologic formation was not very suitable for quarrying underground chambers. All Mycenaean burials in Athens were inhumations, the body being allowed to decompose naturally.

In the so-called 'Dark Ages' following the collapse of Mycenaean civilization, the Agora continued in use as a burial ground, although another important cemetery, located further west in the area of the later Kerameikos, had come into use. Chamber tombs no longer occur. Simple stonelined cist graves are the rule in the earlier (Submycenaean) period, and continue for children in the Protogeometric period (35), but cremation burials in ash-urns (38) become standard for adults.

In addition to archaeological evidence, we may look to Homer for further light on the meaning of funeral practices. Although his date is debated, Homer probably lived in the 8th century, well on in the Geometric period, but his archaeology is not all of one time. He combines practices of his own day with traditions of the heroic Mycenaean age, the memory of which may have been kept alive through oral poetry. For this reason we quote passages from Homer both for the earlier (Mycenaean) and the later (Geometric) burials, with the realization that Homer is poetry and not history.

By combining the archaeological, anthropological, and literary evidence, we hope that this Picture Book may bring to life a few of those ancient Athenians buried beneath, or near, the Agora—the Mycenaean noblewoman (7–16), the warrior with 'imitation silver' vases (20–22), the father and son brought back together from battlefield or hunt (18–19), the baby girl showered with gifts by loving parents (27–28), the wealthy lady with gold earrings and symbolic bridal chest (40–49), and others as well.

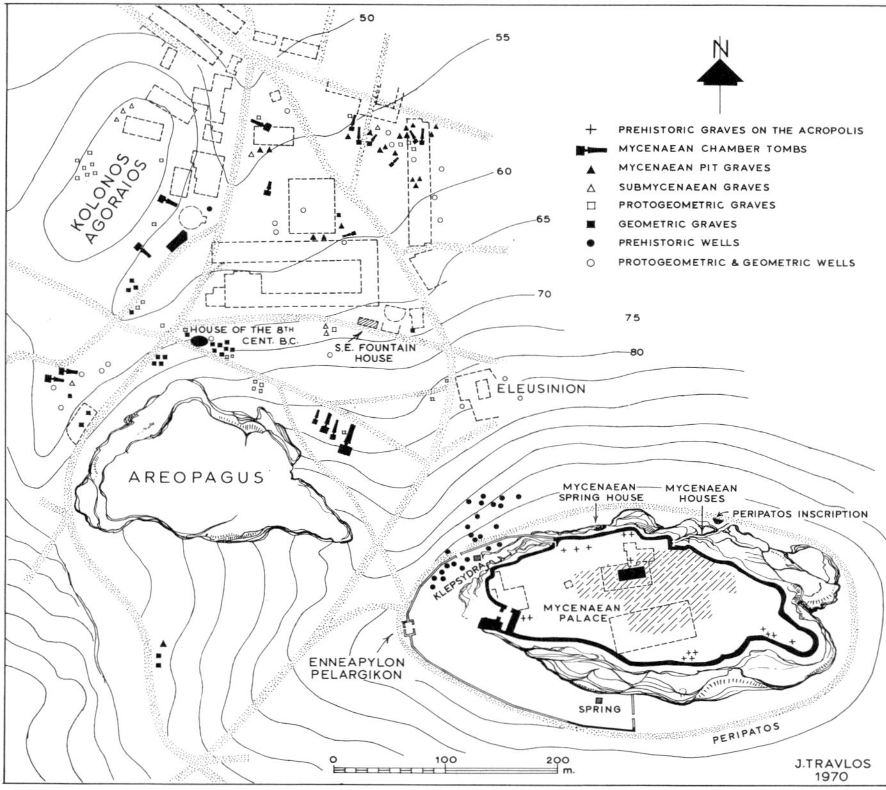

6. Early burials in the Agora and environs.

Chronological Guide
(all dates approximate)

2000–1500 B.C.	Middle Helladic
1500–1400	Early Mycenaean (Late Helladic II or L.H. II)
1400–1200	Mycenaean (L.H. III A and B)
1200–1150	Late Mycenaean (L.H. III C)
1150–1050	Submycenaean
1050–900	Protogeometric
900–850	Early Geometric
850–750	Middle Geometric
750–700	Late Geometric Time of Homer?
700–600	Orientalizing
600	Beginning of Archaic Solon's reforms.

THE TOMB OF A NOBLE ATHENIAN LADY OF ABOUT 1400 B.C.

7. Model of Mycenaean Chamber Tomb, Agora Museum. After the burial the doorway was blocked with stones (to prevent the shade from walking and to keep out robbers) and the entrance passage filled with earth.

IN 1939 the wealthiest Mycenaean chamber tomb ever found in Athens was discovered on the north slope of the Areopagus (2) within a stone's throw of the Acropolis, site of 'the goodly palace of Erechtheus.' Since this was not a built tholos tomb, but a rockcut chamber tomb, it was probably not a royal tomb. However, it must have belonged to a lady of high station, certainly a noblewoman. The size, neat benches, lightly gabled roof, and especially the burial cist with cover slab (8) are exceptional in Athens. Unfortunately the cist was found open with no trace of the body. We can only speculate on what happened. Perhaps the remains were moved to a neighboring tomb after the untimely collapse of the roof. From the mirror, cosmetic boxes, barrettes, etc. we know the occupant was a woman, and the pottery dates the burial to about 1400 B.C.

8. Empty burial cist as found with cover moved aside. Such cists are rare except in royal tombs.

9. Vases and bronze lamp standing beside doorway.

> 'And he set beside him two handled jars of oil and honey leaning them against the bier . . .'
>
> *Iliad*, XXIII, 170–171

Homer thus has Achilles provide for Patroklos on his funeral pyre, since cremation was the standard practice of his own day. However, the jars of oil and honey may represent a continuation of the Mycenaean practice of equipping the dead for the long journey implicit in an inhumation burial. Here in our chamber tomb the two large jars by the doorway (9) must have been filled with provisions for the spirit on its journey to the Other World. The undecorated pointed jar is an import from Canaan (Israel) and may have originally contained myrrh or some other spice shipped wholesale from the Levant; here in its secondary use it probably held wine or oil. The lamp (10) was undoubtedly of practical value to those making the interment, and may have been left symbolically alight by the doorway.

10. Bronze lamp by doorway. It had a conveniently long handle and a small trough in the rim to hold the wick.

11. Vases and ivory cosmetic box on right bench. Found broken by the fall of the rock roof, they are shown after mending, returned to their original position.

12. Large jar with nautilus (argonaut) decoration. Of Cretan shape with a popular marine motive, this vase was made on the Greek mainland about 1400 B.C.

13. The two squat pots seen at the right in 11, here shown one from above, the other in profile. This shape (alabastron) was popular in tombs and probably held perfumed unguents.

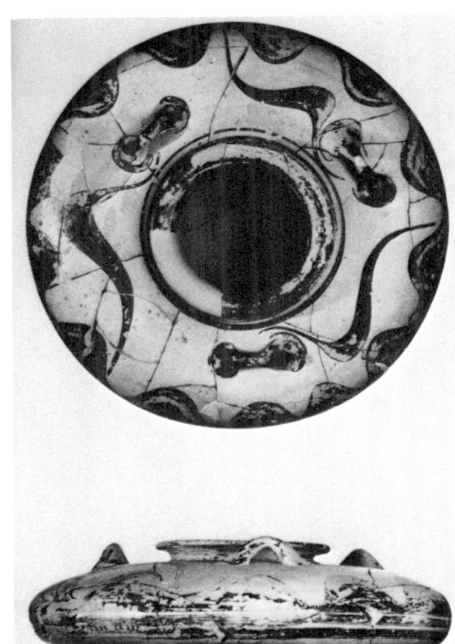

14. Large ivory cosmetic box (pyxis) from bench. Carved in splendid naturalistic style with winged griffins swooping down on young deer, the hollow ivory tusk forms the walls of the box. Fitted with a double bottom and a lid, it also had a tin lining to prevent the rouge or cosmetic from seeping through and staining the ivory.

15. Other feminine articles found near cist (8). The bronze mirror in the center, originally polished, may have been used to apply a cosmetic (eye shadow?) from the small ivory box, lower left. The ivory barrettes at the right are unique, but the straight bone hairpins are common in Mycenaean tombs.

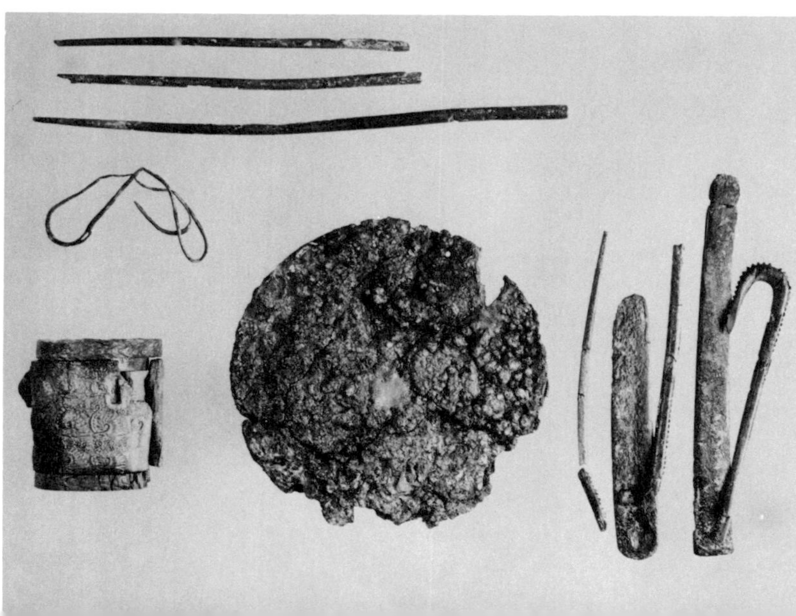

16. Gold ornaments found near burial cist (8).

17. Ivory group from Mycenae.

No valuable gold objects were found in our otherwise rich tomb, and this suggests that whatever jewelry of heavy gold—rings, bracelets, necklace, etc.—our noblewoman wore was removed with her body from the tomb. Over 100 ornaments of thin gold leaf with small perforations and representing rosettes of two sizes, a shell ornament, and an ivy pattern were left behind (16). They may have fallen from her dress, having been sewn to the flounces of a costume which perhaps resembled the court dress worn by the two ladies in the ivory group from Mycenae (17). Although showy, they were hardly valuable enough to retrieve.

18. Remains of two coffin burials in Mycenaean chamber tomb discovered in 1966. These skeletons are A and B in diagram 19. Note position of the large vase (krater, 19, 3 below).

BURIAL IN A FAMILY TOMB

ALTHOUGH the noblewoman's tomb was used only once (and no body was found), Mycenaean chamber tombs were family tombs and were generally used for repeated burials (more than twenty in some cases). Usually the body was deposited directly on the earth floor in an extended or slightly contracted position, and once it became a skeleton—signifying the safe arrival of the soul in the Underworld—it could be shoved aside or the bones deposited in a small pit to make way for subsequent members of the family. This was the customary method, but the Agora has revealed other more exceptional methods—the burial cist with covering slab (8) and here two simultaneous burials made in simple pine boxes or coffins (18–19). Although they had virtually disappeared, fibrous remains of wood above and below the skeletons, A and B, plus the high position of the large krater, supplied the evidence for restoring coffins. Both skeletons were male (father and son?) and were buried on the same day, perhaps brought home from battle or hunt in hastily constructed pine boxes. After an interval the mother, C, and still later, after the ceiling had partially collapsed, the adolescent boy, D, were buried.

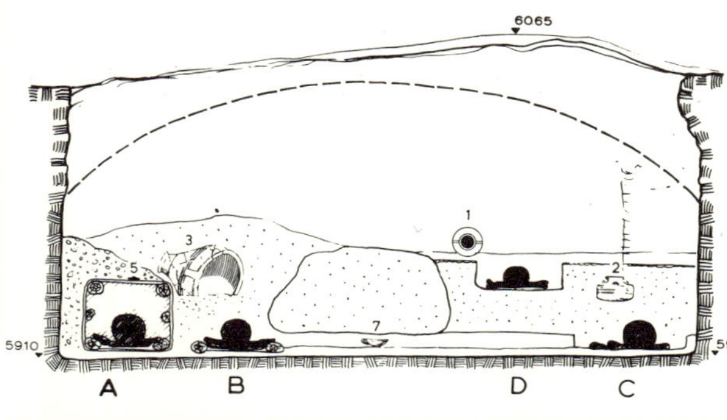

19. Section of tomb above, showing sequence of burials.

TOMB OF A MYCENAEAN WARRIOR OF ABOUT 1350 B.C.

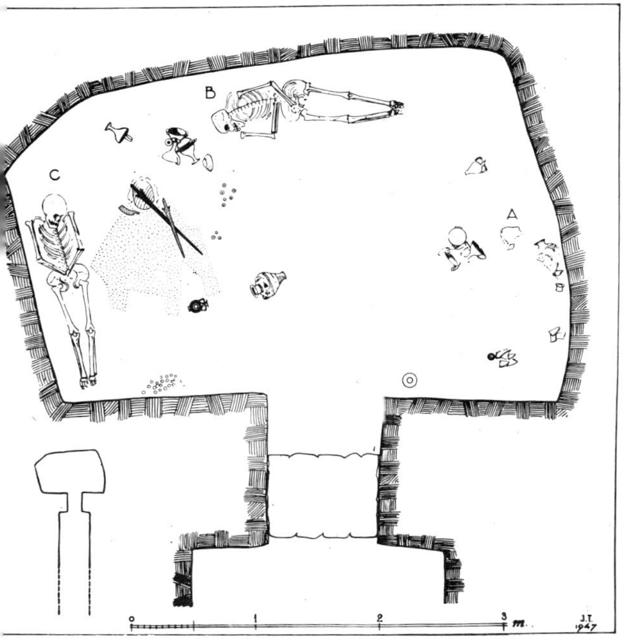

20. Plan of chamber tomb on north slope of Areopagus, near noblewoman's tomb (7). It contained three skeletons, the last, C, a tall man. Beside him on the remains of a wooden table, painted blue and perhaps inlaid with ivory, were his long sword, short sword, and razor (21). The pottery from this tomb was 'imitation silver' (22).

'Across his shoulders he slung the sword with the nails of silver,
a bronze sword . . .'

Iliad, III, 335

THUS HOMER gives us a poetic memory of the long bronze sword or rapier of Mycenaean times, like these with gold-plated rivets (21). In Homer's own day warriors must have used more serviceable iron weapons like those from the Early Geometric warrior's grave (38–39).

21. Bronze swords and razor from wooden table by burial C (20).

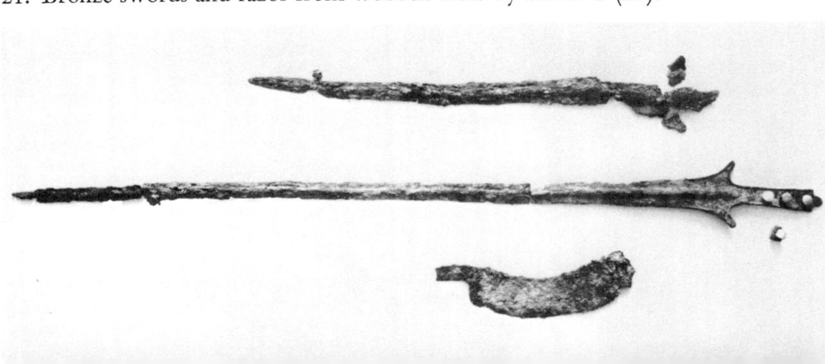

22. 'Imitation silver' service from Mycenaean warrior's tomb. These seven different shapes of stemmed cups, bowls, and pitcher—suitable for funerary offerings of food and drink—were among twelve undecorated vases from this tomb. All preserved traces of a dark coating, chemically analyzed as remnants of tin.

HERE certainly the intention of the tin-coated pottery was to create the impression of a silver service, as the metallic shapes and the existence of a duplicate set of solid silver vases in a tomb in the Argolid indicate. Clearly such a practice was restricted to funerary usage, and although it might seem a cheap trick to play on the dead, it was apparently confined to wealthier burials of the warrior aristocracy. One must remember that tin was rare and had to be imported for the manufacture of bronze. Thus, the 'imitation silver' vases lent status to our warrior, already characterized by his bronze rapier and sword with gold rivets. His burial is second in wealth to that of the noblewoman with the ivory cosmetic boxes. Many Mycenaean burials in the Agora were of a humbler kind, with only a single pot or two. The collection of tools found in one grave (23) is unusual and suggests that their owner was a craftsman.

23. The tools of an artisan. A stone celt, two bone handles, and, in the upper left, half a stone mould for making glass beads. Was this the profession of our humble craftsman?

FROM A STUDY of the anthropological evidence, the skeletons and bones, one realizes the poignant truth that life expectancy was short and many small children did not live beyond the first few years. Epidemics must have taken their toll, as the simultaneous burial of the two little children in a small pit grave (26) would indicate. This burial belongs to the troubled closing years of the Mycenaean age, but in earlier years more thought was lavished upon the little girl of less than two whose fond parents showered her with gifts (27–28). This burial was also made in a small pit grave. In chamber tombs niches were sometimes dug in the entrance passageway for child burials (24). Specific offerings such as feeding bottles (29) or terracotta 'nurses' (30) often accompany child burials.

24. Tomb of the Niches. To avoid shovelling out the dromos and unblocking the door, child burials were made high up in niches, two in the right-hand one, one in the left. Two of the feeding bottles (29) came from this tomb.

25–26. Pit burial of two children of about five and eight (their ages determined by analysis of their teeth). They were buried simultaneously with their heads at opposite ends, and with the cup at left (visible in center of grave) as their only offering.

27–28. Vases and necklace with gold pendant from grave of a little girl, showing feminine finery even for an infant. The two small spouted pots may have served as feeders (see 29). The beautiful Lily Bowl belongs to an early stage of Mycenaean pottery, about 1450 B.C., when the naturalism of Cretan art was still imitated.

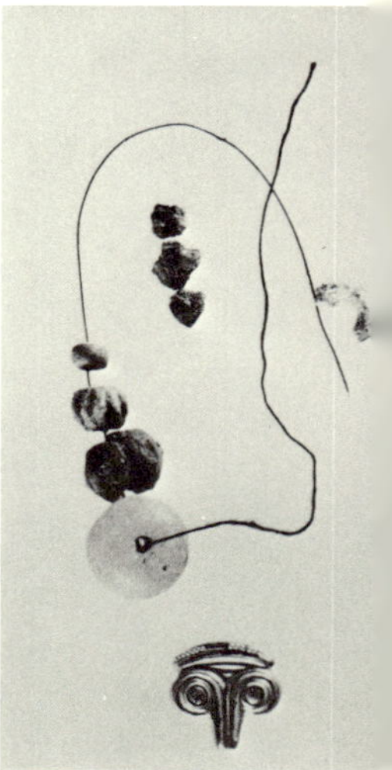

29. Feeding bottles often accompanied Mycenaean child burials (even for children of five or six years). Apparently they were intended to give solace on the long journey to the Underworld. The same shape continued as an infant feeder in the Geometric period (center).

30. Mycenaean 'nurses.' Since these female terracottas occur with child burials, it has been suggested that they also were intended to nourish and care for the little ones on their journey.

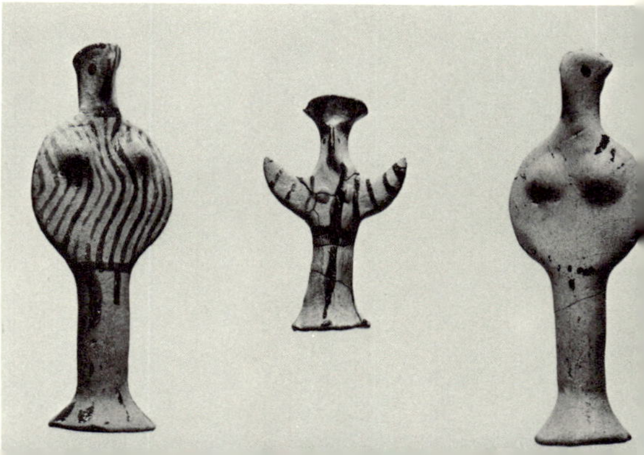

MYCENAEAN FUNERAL RITES

'. . . and nightlong swift-footed Achilleus
from a golden mixing bowl, with a two handled goblet in his hand
drew the wine and poured it on the ground and drenched the ground with it,
and called upon the soul of the unhappy Patroklos.'

Iliad, XXIII, 218 ff.

31. Shattered kylikes, 'two handled goblets,' found in the dromoi of Mycenaean tombs show that a farewell toast was drunk or poured out before the passageway (32) was filled with earth.

'But when the dead man had burned and the dead man's armor, we piled the grave mound and pulled the gravestone to stand above it . . .'

Odyssey, XII, 13–14

ALTHOUGH the passages quoted from Homer refer to cremation funerals of Patroklos and Elpenor, we know that the rites of drinking a toast (and smashing the goblet), heaping up the earth (that is filling the dromos), and erecting some kind of grave marker all go back to the Mycenaean period. In 33 a plain worked stone was used in contrast to the fine carved stele with chariot scene from Mycenae (56). Scraps of animal bones in some tombs suggest a funeral meal like those described by Homer.

32. Entrance passage (dromos) and blocking wall of warrior's tomb (20–22).

33. Fragment of a grave marker from family tomb with coffins (18–19).

MYCENAEAN BURIALS, although usually made in family chamber tombs, were essentially an elaboration of simple inhumations in which the body was deposited in a pit or cist underground and left to decompose naturally, a slow process which led, as we have seen, to the concept of a 'long journey' to the Underworld (see 3–4). This simple method of burial in a rectangular pit or cist, usually covered with several stone slabs, goes back to Middle Helladic times, but persisted in Mycenaean Athens, especially for the burials of children (26) and the less wealthy (34). With the Dark Age period, following the destruction of Mycenaean palaces, simple cist graves replaced family tombs and are characteristic of the new cemeteries on Salamis and in the Kerameikos. The cist became longer and narrower to accommodate an extended burial and was usually lined with stone slabs (35) as well as covered by stones. The example below belongs to the Protogeometric period, in which cremation was the accepted rite for adults, but here the young girl of ten or twelve was buried in an old-fashioned cist grave.

34. Mycenaean cist grave with two cover stones removed. Note the contracted position of the skeleton. A pitcher and jar at the head and a small bronze knife were the only offerings.

35. Protogeometric cist grave of a young girl. Note the extended skeleton and the stone lining. This was a relatively wealthy burial with a number of small pots and simple jewelry.

THE FUNERAL PYRE

'and with the dawn
cause your people to rise, o lord of men Agamemnon,
and bring in timber and lay it by, and all that is fitting
for the dead man to have when he goes down under the gloom and the darkness,
so that with the more speed the unwearying fire may burn him
away from our eyes, and the people turn back to that which they must do.'

Iliad, XXIII, 49–54

THUS ACHILLES ASKS AGAMEMNON to have his people make preparations for the funeral pyre of Patroklos. Likewise Homer's other heroes are cremated in contrast to the inhumations of the Mycenaean age, to which his heroes purportedly belonged. The idea of cremation as a speedy release of the soul from the body was a new one, which the Mycenaeans may have become acquainted with in the Near East at the time of the Trojan War. Nonetheless, it was not until several centuries later that cremation became common, and some of the offerings—such as the symbolic boots for the journey (1 and 37)—may represent a carry-over of idea of appropriate provisions for the long journey implicit in the rite of inhumation.

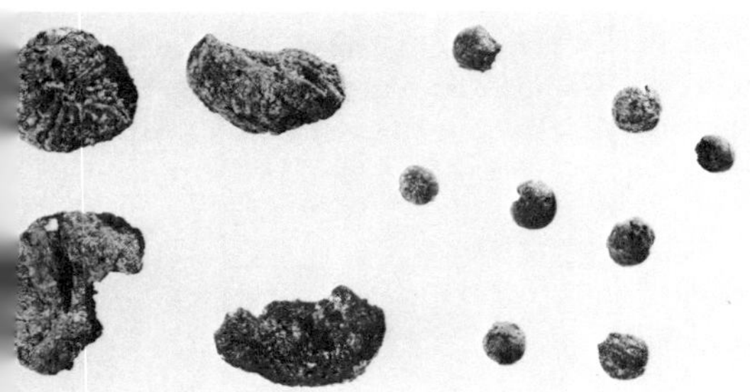

36. Carbonized figs and currants from Early Geometric pyres. Their 'cleansing properties' made them appropriate for funeral banquet and pyre.

37. Part of the funeral offerings from a woman's cremation burial of about 900 B.C.

CREMATION OF A GEOMETRIC WARRIOR OF ABOUT 900 B.C.

38. This drawing shows the vertical section of a Geometric warrior's grave. The large ash-urn (here the characteristic neck amphora preferred for masculine cremations) was covered with a stone and placed in a pit with other offerings which had been burnt on the pyre. The iron sword had first been 'killed' by the fire and was then wrapped around the urn. Carbonized figs and grapes (36) were found in the upper packing under the layer of stones. Located only a few meters away from the contemporary cremation (37), these graves of warrior and woman must belong to one family.

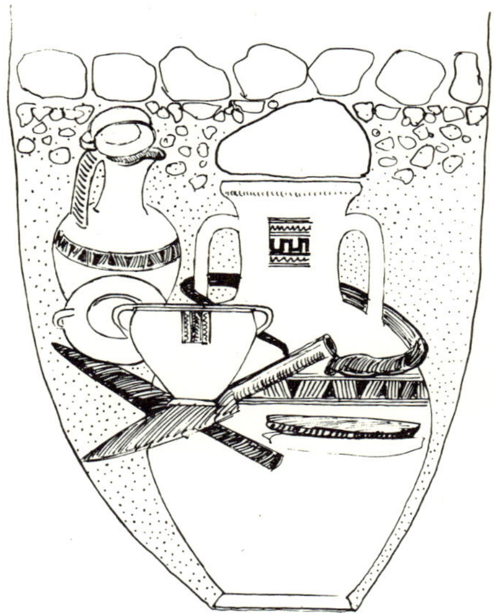

39. Iron weapons and implements from the warrior's cremation. In addition to the long iron sword, his equipment consisted of two spearheads, two knives, a broad axe, a whetstone, and two snaffle bits, the last perhaps of use in chariot races like those depicted on Geometric vases (see 55). Compare these iron weapons with the bronze weapons of the Mycenaean warrior (21) almost 500 years earlier.

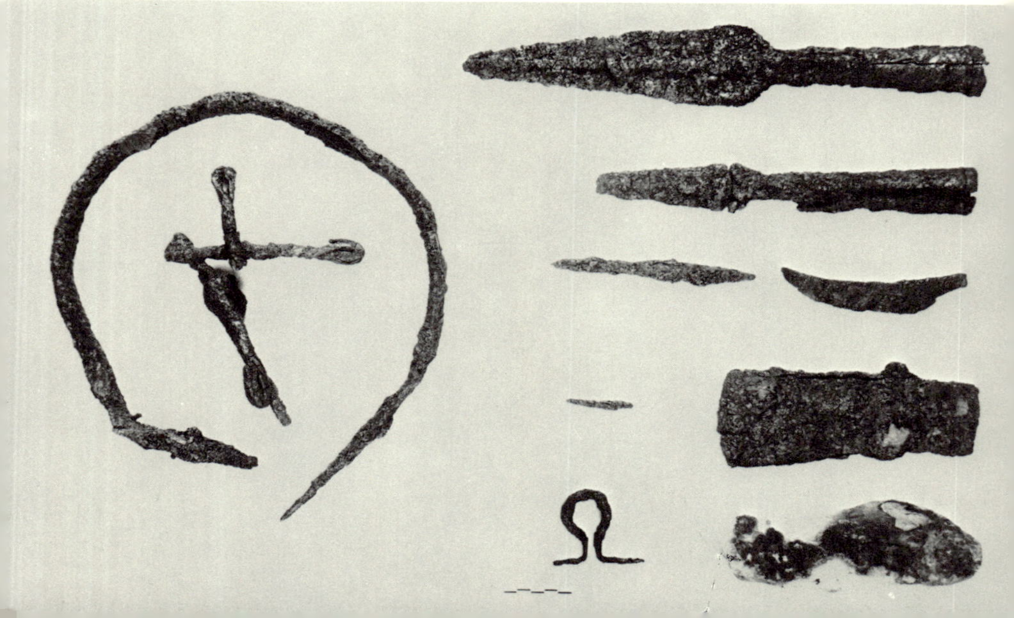

CREMATION BURIAL
OF A RICH ATHENIAN LADY OF ABOUT 850 B.C.

40. Cremation burial as found in 1967. The pit with ash-urn and offerings in center (note chest with granaries, 49), remains of the pyre at left.

NOT FAR down the slope of the Areopagus from the Mycenaean noblewoman's tomb (7–16) discovered some thirty years earlier, an equally exceptional burial of the Geometric period was found in 1967. Although belonging to the same type of urn-hole cremation as the two preceding examples (36–39), this one is far wealthier. The richness of the lady's jewelry (43–45), the symbolism implicit in the chest with five model granaries (49), and the occurrence of exotic imports (45) and techniques (44) suggest a true aristocrat from one of the first Athenian families several centuries before Solon.

41. Geometric vases from urn-hole, a neck amphora, three pitchers, and a covered bowl (pyxis).

'. . . first put out with gleaming wine the pyre that is burning,
all that still has on it the fury of the fire; and afterwards
we shall gather up the bones of Patroklos, the son of Menoitios . . .
And let us lay his bones in a golden jar.'

Iliad, XXIII, 237 ff.

42. Burial urn from cremation grave 40. Not the 'golden jar' requested for Patroklos, but an excellent and serviceable terracotta jar over one-half meter tall decorated in the Early Geometric style of about 850 B.C. Note the panels of Greek fret or meander and the compass-drawn concentric circles with cross fillings in the wide handle zone. This shape, the so-called 'belly-handled amphora,' was common for cremations of women, in contrast to the neck amphora for men (38).

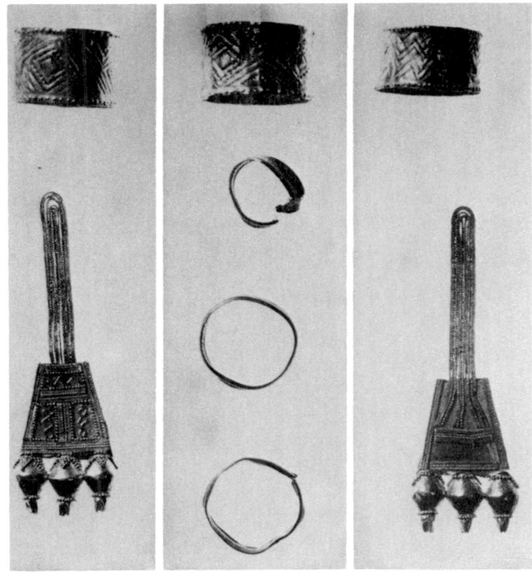

43. Gold jewelry from burial urn. These finger rings and earrings had been removed from the body of the wealthy Athenian lady before cremation; they were then returned to their owner.

44. Detail of gold earring, showing pomegranate pendants (cf. 59). The most elaborate earrings of their period yet found in Greece, they use techniques of twisted gold wire and granulation which show renewed contact with the East, although the form seems purely Greek.

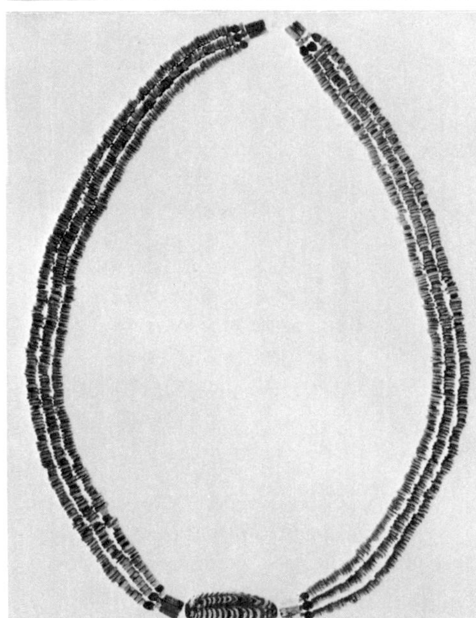

45. Necklace with main strands of blue-green faience. The small beads are brown and white glass; the large bead at the center is green and white, and a rock crystal bead serves as the fastener. The techniques are exotic, and the necklace probably came from a Syrian port.

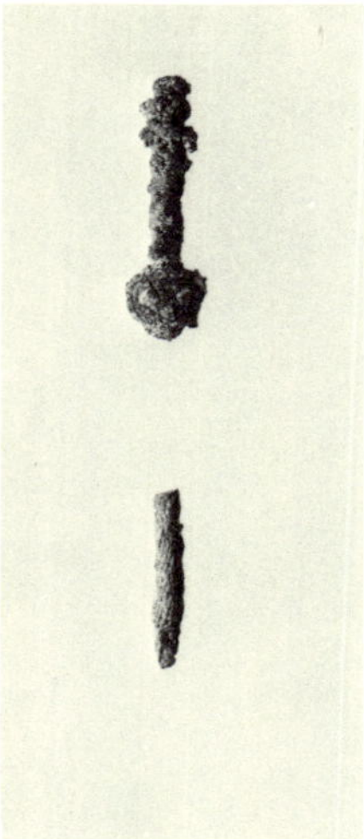
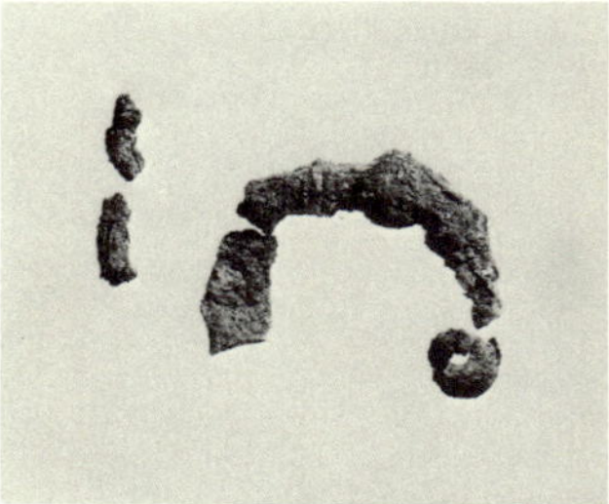

46. Long shoulder pins and safety pin (fibula). The pin at the left is bronze, about twenty centimeters long; the one beside it is iron. These fastened at the shoulders the heavy woolen dress (peplos) like that worn by the Geometric lady below.

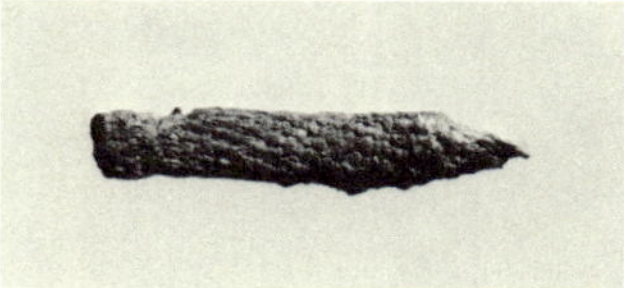

47. Detail of iron pin, showing impressions of woven material.

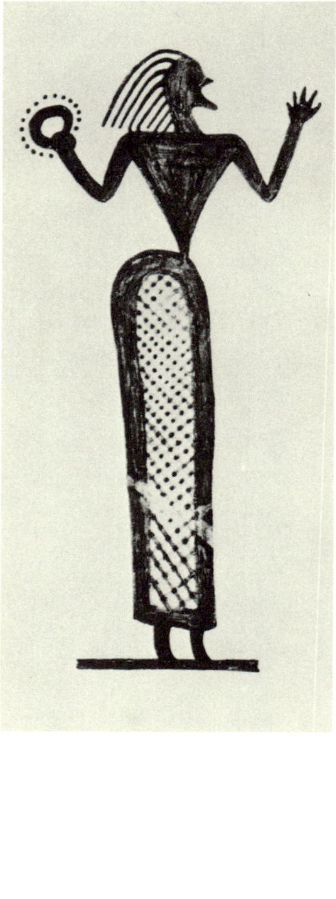

48. Woman on Geometric vase in British Museum. She appears to wear the tight belted peplos of patterned woolen material. It was a simple rectangle pinned at the shoulders with long straight pins and perhaps at the sides with safety pins. Contrast the elaborate sewn costume of the Mycenaean ladies in 17.

49. Terracotta chest with model granaries from urn-hole burial 40. The beehive structures are explained as models of contemporary granaries, in which the grain would have been poured in through the openings at the top, protected by a projecting flap. The two holes at the bottom may have been for ventilation, drawing off the grain, or for the attachment of ladders.

SYMBOLIC OFFERINGS AND STATUS

SYMBOLIC OFFERINGS seem to have increased in the Geometric period. The most elaborate is this unusual terracotta chest from the wealthy female cremation. Although its exact interpretation is debatable, the chest itself seems an imitation of the wooden bridal chest suggesting the married status of the deceased, whereas the five beehive-shaped granaries on the lid may make an allusion to land holdings or property qualifications (anticipating the *pentekosiomedimnoi*, or owners of land producing 500 bushels, of Solon's time?) of her father or husband. The diminutive cutwork terracotta basket (kalathos) in 51, also from this burial, seems to imitate the household wool basket and may symbolize the woman's role in the house. The covered bowl (pyxis) with horses on the lid (50) comes from a somewhat later Geometric woman's grave, also wealthy in its contents. Such pyxides with horses, ranging from one to four, are confined to women's graves; they may also reflect the property status of husband or father.

50. Pyxis with horses on lid from wealthy woman's grave of about 750 B.C.

51. Terracotta model wool basket (kalathos).

WITH THE CHANGE to the rite of cremation for adults, children continued to be buried, sometimes in a cist grave like the young girl of the Protogeometric period (35), sometimes in a large pot or pithos like this sixteen-month-old infant (52). Was this due to the realization that their small bodies would speedily decompose and did not require the expense of the funeral pyre, or was there a natural reluctance to commit them to the fire?

52. Pithos burial of sixteen-month-old infant. The eight small vases below were found within the burial urn, which was covered with a stone slab. Beside the pithos stood a large cooking pot.

53. Miniature vases from Geometric baby's burial. Some were surely made for this purpose, being only five centimeters tall. They belong to the Late Geometric period, about 725 B.C., when birds and curvilinear 'snakes' had replaced the angular ornaments of earlier Geometric (41–42).

MOURNING CUSTOMS

'First among them were Hektor's wife and his honoured mother who tore their hair, and ran up beside the smooth-rolling wagon, and touched his head.'

Iliad, XXIV, 710 ff.

THE PAINTED SCENES on the large Geometric vases from the cemetery in the Kerameikos beyond the Dipylon Gate give us an idea of the mourning customs so poignantly described by Homer, the funeral cortege (*ekphora*) with the dead man on his bier on a wagon surrounded by mourners who tear their hair (54) or the lying-in-state (*prothesis*) which our Cover design reproduces from the famous amphora by the Dipylon Master. The Agora cemetery did not produce any complete examples of these monumental vases, although the smaller amphora overleaf (55) shows a slightly later version of the same themes. Terracotta figurines of mourners (one shown on the title page) from a sacrificial pyre connected with a Late Geometric family cemetery in the Agora (near the later Tholos) are interesting plastic counterparts, the idea of mourning being further reinforced by a painted mourner front and back. We now know from other evidence that the age-old custom of tearing the hair and scratching the face goes back at least to the Mycenaean period.

54. Dipylon krater, Athens, N.M. 990. This vase, over a meter tall, stood as a grave monument in the Dipylon cemetery. It shows on the top row the funeral cortege with the hearse surrounded by a double tier of mourners. The lower scene may represent the chariot race at the funeral games.

'Then all their whips high-lifted above their horses,
they struck with the whip-thongs and in words urged their horses onward
into speed. Rapidly they made their way over the flat land
and presently were far away from the ships.'

Iliad, XXIII, 362 ff.

HOMER in the above passage describes the start of the chariot race at the funeral games which Achilles held in honor of his dead friend Patroklos. From the frequent chariot representations on Dipylon vases (54) we assume that chariot races formed part of the ritual of a Geometric funeral. The practice may even have begun in the Mycenaean period, since chariot scenes occur on sculptured gravestones (56) and on painted vases found in tombs. The Late Geometric amphora (55) from the same family cemetery in the Agora as the mourning terracotta figurine (title page) shows the *prothesis* on the neck and a chariot race on the body.

55. Amphora from the Agora (reconstructed drawing). On this very late Geometri vase (about 700 B.C.) the sloppy drawing contrasts with the neater representations on 54, but the perspe tive is more natural, the tw wheeled chariot being indicated in proper profile. Note the 'whips high-lifte above the horses.'

56. Stele from Mycenae (Athens, N.M. 1428). A more elaborate marker than the plain stone 33, this stood above one of the royal graves in Grave Circle A and dates about 1550 B.C.

WE HAVE MENTIONED a number of symbolic offerings which are ritual in the sense that they served no practical function. Some like the chest with model granaries (49), the pyxis with horses (51), or even the 'imitation silver' service (22), might be thought of as status symbols gratifying the ego of the deceased, or certainly his family. Others, however, have a stronger religious connotation and suggest a belief in an afterlife, or at least in a journey to the Underworld. Among these are the 'nurses' (30) from Mycenaean child burials, the model boots (1, 37) from an Early Geometric cremation, the drink offerings (31) poured out on the earth, or the fruit burnt on the funeral pyre (36). The occurrence of the two ritual vases illustrated below (57, 58) in one Mycenaean tomb and the symbolism of the pomegranate in later Greek religion strongly suggest a belief in some chthonic (Underworld) divinity. In Geometric graves terracotta model pomegranates and pomegranate vases again become popular.

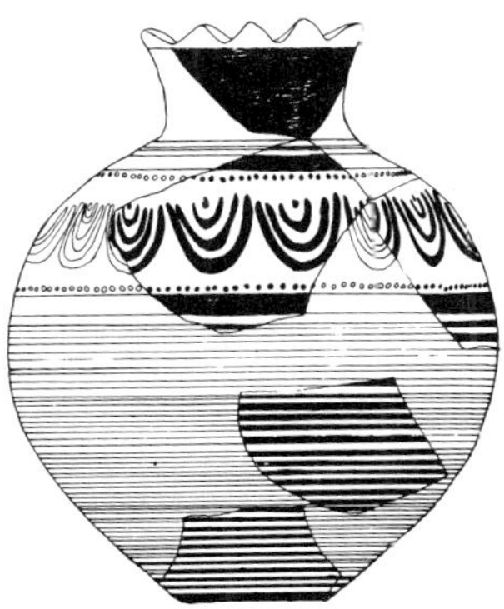

57. Pomegranate vase (reconstructed drawing) found with 58. A unique Mycenaean vase, but known in contemporary faience and glass examples from Egypt, Syria, and Cyprus, whence the fruit and its symbolism may have reached Greece.

58. Mycenaean pot for pouring libations to the dead. A small hole pierced through the base ring allows liquid to trickle slowly out. Another similarly pierced example from Rhodes is decorated with Minoan religious symbols, double axes and 'horns.'

59. Pomegranates on tree (part of Agora replanting). The blood-red juice and many seeds made the fruit an appropriate symbol of life in death and of the Underworld divinities, Demeter and Persephone.

60. Amphora by the Nessos Painter, about 620–610 B.C. The crouching winged sphinx, introduced to Greece during the Orientalizing period, is an interesting precursor of the stone sphinxes on archaic Attic tombstones. (Watercolor.)

THE BURIALS we have considered in some detail span the centuries from about 1450 to 700 B.C., the main period in which our area was used as a cemetery. We know, however, that there must have been earlier Middle Helladic graves destroyed by later building operations. Although the family cemetery on the west side of the Agora near the later Tholos (see 55) came to the end of its use in Late Geometric, about 700 B.C., its precinct wall was respected into the early 6th century, that is down to the time of Solon. By the 7th century, however, the central Agora area had already become too crowded a residential area to permit more burials to be made. The large Sphinx Amphora (60) by the Nessos Painter, which was found in a rockcut shaft near the Hephaisteion, probably stood above a grave on the hill Kolonos Agoraios at the west, and an archaic family cemetery on the northwest slope of the Areopagus (2) continued in use from Late Geometric to the close of the 6th century. After that burials were no longer permitted within the city, although the pyre deposits (62) associated with houses along the borders of the Agora have been interpreted by some as infant cremations.

61. Classical lekythoi from Mycenaean chamber tomb under the later Temple of Ares.

WITH THE ADVENT of Athenian democracy under Solon the Lawgiver in the early 6th century B.C., most of the area of the early cemetery became the civic center, or Agora, for Athens. The early burials, particularly the Mycenaean chamber tombs in the central area, were sometimes encountered by Classical workmen, who twice in the history of one tomb left offerings out of respect for the dead they encountered (61). These were appropriate offerings for their own day, funerary oil jugs (lekythoi) such as would have been used for a mid 5th century B.C. burial. The collection of simple pottery in 62, all with evidence of burning, is typical of a number of pyre or offering deposits found in connection with houses along the borders of the Agora. They are more likely the remains of memorial services to the dead than infant cremations, as has been suggested.

62. Vases from pyre of mid 4th century B.C. The two small pots on the top row are diminutive versions of cooking pots, but the black glazed cup in the center was for actual use. The small plates, saucers, and covered bowl on the lower row are typical of such deposits and may have been used by those participating in the rites.

63. Burial of a pet dog outside the eastern edge of the Agora, behind the Stoa of Attalos (5).

'The stone tells that it contains here the white Maltese dog, Eumelos' faithful guardian. They called him Bull while he still lived, but now the silent paths of night possess his voice.'

Greek Anthology, VII, 211

This epigram reflects the formal burial of a dog with his own gravestone. Sometime during the 4th century B.C. a pet dog was buried just outside the Agora (63). Although he had no tombstone, the miniature pitcher and lamp (64) found with the skeleton as well as a large beef bone 'within sniffing distance' are poignant reminders of the earlier burial practices in this area.

64. Miniature pitcher and lamp from dog's burial. These small offerings would have been appropriate for a human burial of the 4th century B.C.